*Congressional
Research
Service*

The Electoral College: How It Works in Contemporary Presidential Elections

Thomas H. Neale

Specialist in American National Government

October 22, 2012

Congressional Research Service

7-5700

www.crs.gov

RL32611

CRS Report for Congress ───────────────

Prepared for Members and Committees of Congress

Summary

When Americans vote for President and Vice President, they are actually choosing presidential electors, known collectively as the electoral college. It is these officials who choose the President and Vice President of the United States. The complex elements comprising the electoral college system are responsible for one of the most important processes of the American political and constitutional system: election of the President and Vice President. A failure to elect, or worse, the choice of a chief executive whose legitimacy might be open to question, could precipitate a profound constitutional crisis that would require prompt, judicious, and well-informed action by Congress.

Article II, Section 1 of the Constitution, as amended in 1804 by the 12th Amendment, sets forth the requirements for election of the President and Vice President. It authorizes each state to appoint, by whatever means the legislature chooses, a number of electors equal to the combined total of its Senate and House of Representatives delegations, for a contemporary total of 538, including three electors for the District of Columbia. Since the Civil War, the states have universally provided for popular election of the presidential electors. Anyone may serve as an elector, except Members of Congress and persons holding offices of "Trust or Profit" under the Constitution. In each presidential election year, the political parties and other groups that have secured a place on the ballot in each state nominate a "slate" or "ticket" of candidates for elector.

When voters cast a single vote for their favored candidates on general election day, Tuesday after the first Monday in November (November 6 in 2012), they are actually voting for the slate of electors pledged to those candidates. The entire slate of electors winning the most popular votes in the state is elected, a practice known as winner-take-all, or the general ticket system. Maine and Nebraska use an alternative method, the district plan, which awards two electors to the popular vote winners statewide, and one to the popular vote winners in each congressional district. Electors assemble in their respective states on the Monday after the second Wednesday in December (December 17 in 2012). They are expected to vote for the candidates they represent. Separate ballots are cast for President and Vice President, after which the electoral college ceases to exist until the next presidential election. State electoral vote results are reported to Congress and are counted and declared at a joint session of Congress, usually held on January 6 of the year succeeding the election, a date that may be altered by legislation. Since January 6 falls on a Sunday in 2013, Congress will likely set another date for the joint session in 2013, possibly January 8. A majority of electoral votes (currently 270 of 538) is required to win, but the results submitted by any state are open to challenge at the joint session, as provided by law.

Past proposals for change by constitutional amendment have included various reform options and direct popular election, which would eliminate the electoral college system, but no substantive action on this issue has been taken in Congress for more than 20 years. At present, however, a non-governmental organization, the National Popular Vote (NPV) campaign, proposes to reform the electoral college by action taken at the state level; eight states and the District of Columbia have approved the NPV compact to date.

For further information on contemporary proposals to reform or eliminate the electoral college, please consult CRS Report R42139, *Contemporary Developments in Presidential Elections*, by Kevin J. Coleman, R. Sam Garrett, and Thomas H. Neale.

Contents

Figures

Tables

Appendixes

Contacts

Introduction

The President and Vice President of the United States are chosen indirectly by a group of persons elected by American voters. These officials are known as electors, and the institution is referred to collectively as the electoral college. The electoral college, and the system that has grown up around it, are criticized by some as an undemocratic anachronism, and praised by others as a pillar of political stability and the federal system. Absent a constitutional amendment, or the success of non-governmental "reform" initiatives, however, this system will continue to govern U.S. presidential elections for the foreseeable future. While the electoral college has delivered "the people's choice" in 47 of 51 elections since ratification of the 12th Amendment, it can and has delivered Presidents who received fewer popular votes than their major opponents. Moreover, in the highly charged political atmosphere of contemporary presidential elections, a tie vote in the college, the failure of any candidate to receive a majority of electoral votes, or an extremely close election—in either popular or electoral votes—could lead to an acrimonious and protracted political struggle, or even a constitutional crisis. Historically, since ratification of the 12th Amendment, the elections of 1824, 1876, and 1888 revealed the weaknesses of the system, and in the case of 1824 and 1876, arguably brought the nation to the brink of civil violence. More recently, the controversial presidential election of 2000, in which George W. Bush narrowly won the electoral vote and the presidency with fewer popular votes than his major opponent, Al Gore, Jr., continues to influence the tone and content of American political discourse more than a decade later. The potential for a similar or even more bitterly contested struggle in a future election argues for a reasonable level of familiarity with the various components and functions of this complex institution, which this report seeks to provide.

Constitutional Origins

The Constitutional Convention of 1787 considered several methods of electing the President, including selection by Congress, by the governors of the states, by the state legislatures, by a special group of Members of Congress chosen by lot, and by direct popular election. Late in the convention, the matter was referred to the Committee of Eleven on Postponed Matters, which devised the electoral college system in its original form.[1] This plan, which met with widespread approval by the delegates, was incorporated into the final document with only minor changes. As devised by the committee, the electoral college met several standards; it sought to

- reconcile and balance differing state and federal interests;

- give the states, at their discretion, the authority to provide for popular participation in the election, or to retain control of the process within the legislature;

- by providing the "constant two" or "senatorial electors," afford the "smaller" states some additional leverage, so the election process would not be totally dominated by the more populous states;

---

[1] Although the term is not found in the Constitution, the electors have been known collectively as the electoral college since the early days of the republic, an expression that may be misleading, since the college has no continuing existence, never meets in plenary session, and ceases to exist immediately after the electors have performed their function.

- preserve the presidency as independent of Congress for election and reelection; and

- generally insulate the election process from political manipulation.

In the final analysis, the electoral college method of electing the President and Vice President was perhaps the best deal the delegates felt they could get—one of many compromises that contributed to the convention's success. Alexander Hamilton expressed the convention's satisfaction, and perhaps the delegates' relief at the solution they had crafted, when he wrote this of the electoral college in *The Federalist:*

> The mode of appointment of the Chief Magistrate of the United States is almost the only part of the system, of any consequence, which has escaped without severe censure, or which has received the slightest mark of approbation from its opponents.... I venture somewhat further, and hesitate not to affirm that if the manner of it be not perfect, it is at least excellent. It united in an eminent degree all the advantages the union of which was to be wished for.[2]

The Original Constitutional System

The Constitution gave each state a number of electors equal to the combined total of its Senate and House of Representatives membership.[3] The electors were to be chosen by the states "in such Manner as the Legislature thereof may direct" (Article II, Section 1). Qualifications for the office were broad: the only persons prohibited from serving as electors are Senators, Representatives, and persons "holding an Office of Trust or Profit under the United States."[4]

In order to forestall partisan intrigue and manipulation, the electors were required to assemble as separate groups in their respective states and cast their ballots as separate delegations in their respective states, rather than meet as a body in a single location.

At least one of the candidates for whom the electors voted was required to be an inhabitant of another state. This was intended to counter what the framers feared would be a provincial insularity once George Washington, the indispensable figure who, it was universally assumed, would be the first President, had left the political scene. By requiring one of the candidates to be from somewhere else, the convention delegates hoped to prod the electors to look beyond the borders of their own state or region in search of presidential timber.

A number of votes equal to a majority of the whole number of electors was necessary to elect. This requirement was intended to insure that the winning candidate enjoyed broad support, while election by the House of Representatives was provided as a default method in the event of electoral college deadlock. Finally, Congress was empowered to set nationwide dates for choice and meeting of electors.

---

[2] Alexander Hamilton, "The Method of Electing the President," in *The Federalist*, number 68 (Cambridge, MA: Belknap Press of Harvard U. Press, 1966), p. 440.

[3] A map and table portraying the current allocation of electoral votes among the states may be found in the **Appendix** to this report, on pages 19-21.

[4] U.S. Constitution, Article II, Section 1, clause 2.

The 12ᵗʰ Amendment Repairs Flaws in the Original System

The original method of electing the President and Vice President, however, proved unworkable. Under this system, each elector cast two votes for two different candidates for the office of *President*, but no votes for *Vice President*. The candidate who received the most electoral votes was elected, provided he received a number of votes equal to a majority of the whole number of *electors*—not a majority of *electoral votes*. Nobody actually ran for Vice President—the runner-up in the presidential contest was elected to the second office. This system, which was intended to bring the two best qualified candidates to office, never anticipated the early growth of political parties and factions, each of which offered a joint ticket of two candidates—one for President and one for Vice President.

By the third election, in 1796, the nascent political parties of the day, Federalists and anti-Federalists (also known as Jeffersonians or Republicans[5]), each offered a joint ticket. Under the original arrangement, the only way to make the system work was for all of the party's electors to cast one of their two votes for the recognized presidential candidate, and all *but one* of the electors cast their second votes for the vice presidential candidate. One elector would be instructed to withhold his second vote for the designated vice presidential candidate, so that the two candidates would not tie the vote and throw the election to the House.

This cumbersome system broke down almost immediately, in 1800, when a Republican elector failed to withhold his second vote from the acknowledged vice presidential candidate. This led to a tie between presidential candidate Thomas Jefferson and his running mate, Aaron Burr, leaving the election to be decided in the House of Representatives. The constitutional crisis resulting from the election of 1800 led to the 12ᵗʰ Amendment, which was proposed by Congress and speedily ratified by the states, as noted later in this report.[6]

The Electoral College Today[7]

Notwithstanding the founders' efforts, the electoral college system almost never functioned as they intended, but, as with so many constitutional provisions, the document prescribed only the system's basic elements, leaving ample room for development. As the republic evolved, so did the electoral college system, and, by the late 19ᵗʰ century, the following range of constitutional, federal and state legal, and political elements of the contemporary system were in place.

---

[5] To avoid confusion, it should be noted that the "Jeffersonian" or "Republican" proto-party of the 1790s was the ancestor of the modern Democratic Party. The modern Republican Party, which also claimed descent from the Jeffersonians, emerged in the 1850s.

[6] For further information on the election of 1800 and the 12ᵗʰ Amendment, consult Neal R. Peirce and Lawrence D. Longley, *The People's President, The Electoral College in American History and the Direct Vote Alternative*, revised edition (New Haven, CT: Yale University Press, 1981), pp.36-44.

[7] For information on proposals to reform the electoral college, see CRS Report R42139, *Contemporary Developments in Presidential Elections*, by Kevin J. Coleman, R. Sam Garrett, and Thomas H. Neale; and CRS Report R42139, *Contemporary Developments in Presidential Elections*, by Kevin J. Coleman, R. Sam Garrett, and Thomas H. Neale.

Who Are the Electors?[8]

The Constitution, as noted earlier in this report, states what the electors *may not be*; that is, it prohibits Senators, Representatives, and persons holding an "Office of Trust or Profit under the United States" from serving. In effect, this language bars not only Members of the two houses of Congress, but any person who is an employee of the United States government—justices, judges, and staff of the U.S. courts and the federal judiciary; all political employees of the legislative and executive branches; federal professional civilian employees—"civil servants;" and U.S. military and law enforcement personnel.[9]

In practice, the two major political parties tend to nominate a mixture of well-known figures such as governors and other state and local elected officials, party activists, local and state celebrities, and "ordinary" citizens for the office of elector.

While they may be well-known persons, electors generally receive little recognition as such. In fact, in most states, the names of individual elector-candidates do not appear anywhere on the ballot; instead only those of the presidential and vice presidential candidates appear, sometimes prefaced by the words "electors for." Moreover, electoral votes are commonly referred to as having "been awarded" to the winning candidate, as if no human beings were involved in the process.

Nominating Elector-Candidates: Diverse State Procedures

The Constitution and federal law are silent on nomination procedures for elector-candidates, so the process of nominating elector-candidates is another of the many aspects of this system left to state and political party preferences. Most states prescribe one of two methods: 32 states and the District of Columbia provide by law that major party candidates for presidential elector be nominated by state party conventions, while five states provide by law for nomination by the state party's central committee. The remainder use a variety of methods, including unspecified party option, nomination by the governor (on recommendation of party committees), by primary election, and by the party's presidential nominee. Provisions governing new and minor political parties, as well as independent candidacies, are generally prescribed in state law, and are even more widely varied.[10]

---

[8] For a list of electors in the presidential election of 2008, consult the National Archives and Records Administration's website at http://www.archives.gov/federal-register/electoral-college/2008-certificates/.

[9] It is unclear whether the constitutional prohibition covers persons who serve without compensation on federal executive or congressional advisory boards and commissions. A 2007 opinion for the General Counsel of the Federal Bureau of Investigation (FBI) held that members of the FBI Director's Advisory Board should not be considered to hold an "Office Profit or Trust" under the United States, as described in the Constitution's so-called emoluments clause (Article I, Section 9, clause 8). From this opinion, it could be inferred that members of the said boards and commissions would not be covered by the Article II, Section 1, clause 2 prohibiting persons holding "an Office of Trust or Prophet" from serving as presidential electors. For further information, consult "Application of the Emoluments Clause to a Member of the Federal Bureau of Investigation Director's Advisory Board," Memorandum Opinion for the General Counsel, Federal Bureau of Investigation, June 15, 2007. Available to Members of Congress and their staff from the author of this report.

[10] For information on elector-nomination procedures in the individual states, please consult: U.S. Congress, *Nomination and Election of the President and Vice President of the United States, 2008*, 111th Congress 2nd sess., S. Doc. 111-15 (Washington: GPO, 2010), pp. 346-428. This is the most recent edition available in 2012.

How Are Electoral Votes Allocated Among the States?

The Constitution gives each state a number of electors equal to the combined total of its Senate membership (two for each state) and House of Representatives delegation (currently ranging from one to 53, depending on population). The 23rd Amendment provides an additional three electors to the District of Columbia. The total number of electoral votes per state, based on the most recent (2010) census, ranges from three, for seven states and the District of Columbia, to 55 for California, the most populous state. **Figure A-1** and **Table A-1** in the appendix of this report provide current electoral vote allocations by state and D.C. for the elections of 2012, 2016, and 2020.

These totals are adjusted following each decennial census in a process called reapportionment, which reallocates the number of Members of the House of Representatives to reflect changing rates of population growth (or decline) among the states.[11] Thus, a state may gain or lose electors following reapportionment, as it gains or loses Representatives, but it always retains its two "senatorial" electors, and at least one more reflecting its House delegation. The current allocation among the states is in effect for the presidential elections of 2012, 2016, and 2020; electoral votes will next be reallocated following the 2020 census, an alignment that will be in effect for the 2024 and 2028 elections.

How Are the Electors Chosen?

The Constitution specifically grants the right to decide how electors will be *chosen*—as opposed to being *nominated*—to the legislatures of the several states:

> Each State shall appoint, in such Manner as the Legislature thereof may direct, a Number of Electors, equal to the whole Number of Senators and Representatives to which the State may be entitled in the Congress.[12]

Today, all presidential electors are chosen by the voters, but, in the early Republic, more than half the states chose electors by votes of the legislators in their legislatures, thus eliminating any direct involvement by the voting public in the election. This practice changed rapidly after the turn of the 19th century, however, as the right to vote was extended to an ever-wider segment of the population, culminating in the extension of the franchise to all eligible citizens 18 years of age or older. The tradition that the voters choose the presidential electors thus became a permanent feature of the electoral college system quite early in the history of the republic.[13]

While the vote for electors has devolved to individuals, the constitutional power of the state legislatures to decide how the electors will be chosen remains essentially unimpaired.[14] This was

---

[11] For additional information on the apportionment process, please consult CRS Report R41357, *The U.S. House of Representatives Apportionment Formula in Theory and Practice*, by Royce Crocker.

[12] U.S. Constitution, Article II, Section 1, clause 2.

[13] Peirce and Longley, *The People's President*, revised edition, pp. 44-47.

[14] The legislature's power is, however, subject to certain constitutional constraints, particularly if state procedures are found to have violated the equal protection clause of the 14th Amendment. For additional information, please consult U.S. Congress, Senate, *The Constitution of the United States, Analysis and Interpretation*, "Article II, Section 1, clauses 2-4," 108th Cong., 2nd sess., Sen. Doc. 108-17 (Washington: GPO, 2004), pp. 450-452. Also available online at http://www.gpo.gov/fdsys/search/pagedetails.action?granuleId=GPO-CONAN-2002-8-3&packageId=GPO-CONAN-2002&fromBrowse=true.

---

illustrated as recently as 2000. During the political struggle that followed that year's presidential election in Florida, it was suggested that the state's legislature might step in to appoint electors if local election authorities and state courts were unable to determine who had won its 25 electoral votes by the deadline required by federal law (this so-called "Safe Harbor" provision is examined later in this report). Although many commentators asserted that a return to selection of electors by the state legislature would be an unacceptable retreat from democratic practices, no serious arguments were raised against the constitutional right of the Florida legislature to do so.[15]

The Electors' Task: Ratifying the Voters' Choice

Presidential electors in contemporary elections are expected, and, in many cases pledged, to vote for the candidates of the party that nominated them. While there is considerable evidence that the founders assumed they would be independent, weighing the merits of competing presidential candidates, the electors have been regarded as agents of the public will since the first decade under the Constitution.[16] They are expected to vote for the candidates of the party that nominated them. "Faithless" electors provide an occasional exception to that accepted rule.

Disregarding the Voters' Choice: Faithless Electors

Notwithstanding the tradition that electors are bound to vote for the candidates of the party that nominated them, individual electors have sometimes broken their commitment, voting for a different candidate or candidates other than those to whom they were pledged; they are known as "faithless" or "unfaithful" electors. Although 24 states seek to prohibit faithless electors by a variety of methods, including pledges and the threat of fines or criminal action,[17] most constitutional scholars believe that once electors have been chosen, they remain constitutionally free agents, able to vote for any candidate who meets the requirements for President and Vice President.[18] Faithless electors have been few in number (since the 20th century, one each in 1948, 1956, 1960, 1968, 1972, 1976, and 1988[19], one blank ballot cast in 2000,[20] and one in 2004[21]), and have never influenced the outcome of a presidential election.

---

[15] "Florida Legislative Leaders Call Special Session for Friday," CNN Politics, December 6, 2000, CNN.com, December 11, 2000, available at http://articles.cnn.com/2000-12-06/politics/fla.legislature_1_special-session-senate-president-john-mckay-electoral-votes?_s=PM:ALLPOLITICS; and Jim Saunders and Randolph Pendleton, "Legislators Poised to Pick Bush Electors," *Florida Times Union/Jacksonville.com*, December 12, 2000, available at http://jacksonville.com/tu-online/stories/121200/met_4857971.html; and John C. Fortier, ed., *After the People Vote, A Guide to the Electoral College*, third edition, (Washington: AEI Press, 2005), p. 45.

[16] Peirce and Longley, *The People's President*, revised edition, pp. 24, 96-101.

[17] For information on these restrictions, please consult: U.S. Congress, *Nomination and Election of the President and Vice President of the United States, 2008*, pp. 346-428. This is the most recent edition available in 2012.

[18] U.S. Congress, Senate, *The Constitution of the United States of America, Analysis and Interpretation*, pp. 453-455. Also available in PDF format at http: http://www.gpo.gov/fdsys/pkg/GPO-CONAN-2002/pdf/GPO-CONAN-2002-8-3.pdf.

[19] For the names of faithless electors and the circumstances under which they cast their votes, see http://archive.fairvote.org/e_college/faithless.htm.

[20] For the name of the elector and the circumstances under which this elector cast a blank electoral vote ballot in 2000, see http://archive.fairvote.org/e_college/faithless.htm.

[21] In 2004, one Minnesota elector cast votes for John Edwards for both President and Vice President. No objection was raised in the January 6, 2005, joint session at which electoral votes were counted, and the vote was recorded as cast. See National Archives and Records Administration website at http://www.archives.gov/federal-register/electoral-college/scores2.html#2004.

General Election Ballots

General election ballots, which are regulated by state election laws and authorities, offer voters joint candidacies for President and Vice President for each political party or other group. That is, voters cast a single vote for electors pledged to the joint ticket of the presidential and vice presidential nominees of the party they represent. This practice conforms to the Constitution, which provides for only one set of electors, although the electors vote separately for President and Vice President. This practice also eliminates the possibility that voters could pick and choose among electors from different parties.

Most states do not print the names of individual elector-candidates on the general election ballot. The most common variants are for only the names and party identification of the presidential and vice presidential nominees to appear on the ballot, in some cases preceded by the phrase "Electors for." Some states further specify in law that a vote for these candidates is a vote for the elector-candidates of that party or other political group.[22]

Winner Take All: How the General Ticket System Awards the Electoral Vote in Most States

While the Constitution is silent on the exact procedure for awarding each state's electoral votes, 48 states and the District of Columbia currently use the "general ticket" or "winner-take-all" system. The sole exceptions to this practice, Maine and Nebraska, use the "district" system, which is examined later in this report. Under the general ticket system, each political party or group or independent candidacy that is eligible to be placed on the ballot nominates a group (also known as "ticket" or "slate") of candidates for the office of elector equal in number to the state's total number of electors. As noted previously, voters then cast a single vote for the presidential and vice presidential candidates of their choice; when they do so, they actually cast a vote for the entire ticket of electors *pledged* to the candidates of their choice. The ticket receiving the most votes statewide (a plurality is sufficient) is elected. These people become the electors for that state.

As an illustration, this is how the general ticket system works in a hypothetical state, "State A." Assume that State A currently has 10 electoral votes, reflecting its two Senators and eight Representatives. The two equally hypothetical major parties, "Party X" and "Party Y" each nominate 10 persons for the office of presidential elector, pledged to the presidential and vice presidential candidates of their party. Voters go to the polls and cast a single vote for the ticket of party electors of their choice, although as noted previously, only the names of the presidential and vice presidential candidates are likely to appear on the ballot. Party X's slate of elector-candidates receives 51% of the popular vote; Party Y's slate receives 49%. Notwithstanding the closeness of the results, all 10 of Party X's electors are chosen, and Party Y wins no electoral votes in the state. The Party X electors are pledged to their party's presidential and vice presidential candidates, and they normally vote to confirm the choice of the citizens who elected them (the exception, as noted previously, would be the infrequent faithless elector).

The general ticket system has been favored since the 19th century, as it tends to magnify the winning candidates' victory margin within states and across the nation, and generally guarantees a

---

[22] For information on individual state ballot format, please consult: U.S. Congress, *Nomination and Election of the President and Vice President of the United States, 2008*, pp. 346-428. This is the most recent edition available in 2012.

national electoral college majority for the winners. It has, however, been criticized on the grounds that it effectively negates the votes for the runners-up. Returning to State A, some critics suggest that it would be more equitable, given the state of the popular vote, if a number of electors supporting Party Y's candidate were chosen. Alternative methods of allocating electors are examined in a later section of this report, under ""Mend It" — Reforming the Electoral College."

General Election Day

Elections for all federal elected officials are held on the Tuesday after the first Monday in November in even-numbered years; presidential elections are held in every year divisible by four (November 6, for the 2012 presidential election). Congress selected this day in 1845;[23] previously, states held elections on different days between September and November, a practice that sometimes led to multiple voting across state lines, and other fraudulent practices. By mandating a single presidential election day, Congress sought to eliminate such irregularities.

Other factors also contributed to Congress's choice of a November election day. By tradition, November was chosen because the harvest was in, and farmers had some leisure time, and thus were able to take the time needed to vote. Tuesday was selected because it gave a full day's travel between Sunday, which was widely observed as a strict day of rest, and election day.[24] The choice of Tuesday after the first Monday also meant that election day would never fall on the first day of the month, which was generally the day on which local courts convened. This was intended to avoid congestion at the county seat. Finally, travel was also easier throughout the northern states during November, before winter had set in.

The Electors Convene

The 12th Amendment requires electors to meet "in their respective states." This provision was intended by the founders to deter "intrigue" and manipulation of the election by having the state electoral colleges meet simultaneously, but in separate locations. Congress by law sets the date on which the electors meet, which is currently the first Monday after the second Wednesday in December (December 17, 2012).[25] The same law set the "safe harbor" provision, whereby in cases of disputed state results, if the said state has provided a means of resolving disputes prior to election day, and if this means has been used to reach a decision as to the election result not less than six days before the date on which the electors are scheduled to meet, then that decision is final.[26] The electors almost always meet in the state capital, usually in the capitol building or state house itself. They vote "by ballot"—paper ballot [27]—separately for President and Vice President. At least one of the candidates must be from another state, a provision retained from the original constitutional provisions; as noted earlier, it was intended by the founders to promote the

---

[23] Statutes at Large, 5 Stat. 721.

[24] In most rural areas, the only polling place was at the county seat, frequently a full day's journey for voters from the further reaches of a county.

[25] 3 U.S.C. 7.

[26] This requirement, found at 3 U.S.C. (5), was crucial in decisive allocation of Florida's electors in the 2000 presidential election.

[27] 12th Amendment. This provision has historically been interpreted to require paper ballots for President and Vice President.

selection of nationally renowned candidates, and to prevent the electors from selecting exclusively "native sons."

The results are then endorsed, and copies are sent to the following officials:

- the Vice President of the United States (in his capacity as President of the Senate);

- the state secretary of state or the comparable state officer;

- the Archivist of the United States; and

- the judge of the federal district court of the district in which the electors met.[28]

The electors then adjourn, and the electoral college ceases to exist until the next presidential election.

Congress Counts, Ascertains, and Declares the Vote

Aside from the presidential inauguration on January 20, the final step in the presidential election process is the counting, ascertainment, and declaration of the electoral votes in Congress.[29] The House of Representatives and the Senate meet in joint session in the House chamber on January 6 of the year following the presidential election. Since January 6 falls on a Sunday in 2013, it is anticipated that Congress will set a different date, possibly January 8, for the joint session.[30] No debate is allowed in the joint session. The Vice President, who presides in his capacity as President of the Senate, opens the electoral vote certificates from each state, in alphabetical order. He then passes the certificates to four tellers (vote counters), two appointed by the House, and two by the Senate, who announce the results. The votes are then counted, and the results are announced by the Vice President. The candidates receiving a majority of electoral votes, currently 270 of 538, are declared the winners by the Vice President, an action that constitutes "a sufficient declaration of the persons, if any, elected President and Vice President of the States."[31]

Objections to State Electoral Vote Returns

Objections may be offered to both individual electoral votes and state returns as a whole. Objections must be filed in writing, and be signed by one U.S. Senator and one Representative. If an objection is received in the joint session, and is determined to be valid, then the electoral vote count session is recessed. The Senate returns immediately to its chamber, and the two houses of Congress consider the objections separately. By law,[32] these sessions cannot last more than two hours, and no Member of either house may speak for more than five minutes. At the end of this period, the houses vote separately to agree or disagree with the objection. The Senate then returns to the House chamber, and the joint session reconvenes. The decisions of the two houses are

---

[28] 3 U.S.C. 11.

[29] 3 U.S.C. 15-18.

[30] This action is usually accomplished by a joint resolution originating in the House. For the 2009 joint session, for instance, the date was set by H.J.Res. 100, 110th Congress. At the time of this writing, no resolution concerning the date for the joint session has been introduced in the 112th Congress.

[31] 3 U.S.C. 15.

[32] 3 U.S.C. 17.

announced. If both houses agree to the objection, then the electoral vote or votes in question are not counted. Otherwise, the vote or votes stand as submitted, and are counted as such.[33]

This process was most recently used following the 2004 presidential election. An objection was raised to the certificate of the electoral vote filed by the State of Ohio at the joint electoral count session held on January 6, 2005. It met the required standards, being submitted in writing, and bearing the signatures of one Representative and one Senator. The joint session was duly recessed, and the two houses of Congress reconvened separately to debate and vote on the objection, which they rejected. The certificate of electoral votes submitted by Ohio was accepted, and the vote was duly recorded.[34]

A Tie or Failure to Win a Majority in the Electoral College: Contingent Election by Congress

The 12th Amendment, as noted earlier in this report, requires that candidates receive a majority of electoral votes, at least 270 of the current total of 538, in order to be elected President or Vice President. In the event of a tie, or if no candidate receives a majority, then choice of the President and Vice President "defaults" to Congress in a procedure known as contingent election.[35] In a contingent election, the House of Representatives elects the President, choosing from among the *three* candidates who received the most electoral votes. The Senate elects the Vice President in a contingent election, choosing between the *two* candidates who received the largest number of electoral votes.

Perhaps the most notable feature of contingent election is that each state has the same vote, regardless of population. In the House, each state delegation casts a single vote for President, while in the vice presidential election, each Senator casts a single vote.

2012 Presidential Election: An Electoral College Timeline

May-August 2012 — State party organizations nominate a ticket of candidates for elector for President and Vice President in their states.

November 6, 2012 — General Election Day. Voters cast one ballot for the joint ticket of their preferred candidates for President and Vice President. These are actually votes for the electors committed to the candidates they represent.

December 11, 2012 — The "Safe Harbor" deadline. As noted earlier, if, on or before election day, a state shall have provided by law for determination of controversies or contests over the electors

---

[33] For further information on proceedings at joint electoral vote counting sessions of Congress, please consult CRS Report RL32717, *Counting Electoral Votes: An Overview of Procedures at the Joint Session, Including Objections by Members of Congress*, by Jack Maskell and Elizabeth Rybicki.

[34] For the proceedings at the joint count session of January 6, 2005, please consult *Congressional Record*, volume 151, part 1, January 6, 2005, pp. 157-173, 197-243.

[35] For further information, see CRS Report R40504, *Contingent Election of the President and Vice President by Congress: Perspectives and Contemporary Analysis*, by Thomas H. Neale.

and electoral votes, and if these procedures have been applied, and results have been determined on or before this date, these results shall be conclusive, and shall govern in the counting of the electoral votes.

December 17, 2012 — The electoral college meets. State delegations of electors meet separately in their respective states at a place designated by the state legislature. In practice, the electors usually meet in the state capital, often in the state house or capitol building. The electors vote "by ballot" — paper ballot — for President and Vice President. Certificates of the results are then transmitted to the President of the U.S. Senate (one copy), the Archivist of the United States (two copies), the secretary of state or equivalent officer of the state in which the electors met (two copies), and the judge of the U.S. district court of the district in which the electors met (one copy).

December 26, 2012 — Certificates must be delivered to the officers specified above not later than this date.

January 6, 2013 — On this date, or another date designated by Congress, the Senate and House of Representatives assemble in joint session to count the electoral votes. The announcement of the state of the vote is deemed sufficient declaration of the persons elected President and Vice president.

Red States, Blue States, Battleground States

For the general public, perhaps the most widespread contemporary electoral college imagery centers on the "Red State/Blue State" and "Battleground States" characterizations that have emerged in mass media in recent years.

"Red State/Blue State" in contemporary political language provides a heuristic for defining a state's political record and voting pattern. Although there are always exceptions to the rules, Red states are generally considered to be those expected to favor the Republican candidates, while blue states tend to vote Democratic. According to press accounts, the categorization of states as "Red" or "Blue" originated during the presidential election campaign of 2000. Although national television networks had favored red and blue for their election-night electronic maps of the states for at least 20 years, they had not previously associated particular colors with either party on a consistent basis from election to election.[36] NBC television journalist Tim Russert is generally credited with making the first nationwide reference to "red states" and "blue states," in remarks he made during an October 30, 2000, broadcast of "Meet the Press."[37] The phrase quickly gained currency, and has since become a standard verbal identifier for defining a state's political record and voting patterns. The red state/blue state label is also often used to identify a state's political history over the longer run: Texas, which has voted for Republican presidential candidates in every election since 1972, is generally typed as a red state, while California, which has voted Democratic in every presidential election since 1988, is considered to be a blue state. A more recent addition to the political spectrum is the "purple state,"[38] one which is closely contested by

---

[36] Paul Farhi, "Elephants Are Red, Donkeys Are Blue, Colors Are Sweet, So States Have Their Hue," *Washington Post*, November 2, 2004, p. C1, available at: http://www.washingtonpost.com/wp-dyn/articles/A17079-2004Nov1.html.

[37] Ibid.

[38] In the visible spectrum, purple falls between red and blue, and is often considered a blend of the two.

the competing parties; Ohio and Colorado have been characterized as purple states.[39] Purple status can also be used to identify a state whose voters may be trending away from previous voting patterns to support of a different party. For example, Virginia, which voted Democratic in the 2008 presidential election for the first time since 1964, has been characterized by some commentators as a red state that may be trending from red to purple. [40]

The terms "Battleground States" and "Swing States" are generally used to identify those in which the major parties are closely matched, and which are less predictable in their presidential choices from election to election. In all but the most lopsided presidential election campaigns, the electoral votes controlled by battleground states will provide the margin of victory for the winning candidates. Presidential campaign organizations, therefore, generally direct a high proportion of funds and resources to winning the vote in battleground states. Similarly, the candidates spend more time campaigning in these states than they would in states where they enjoy solid margins of support.[41] This concentration of resources in the battleground states has been criticized by opponents of the electoral college system as short-changing the great majority of states and voters in terms of campaign attention and candidate visits:

> In 2004 and 2008, candidates concentrated two-thirds of their visits and ad money in the post-convention campaign in just six closely divided "battleground" states—with 98% going to just 15 states. The net effect is that two-thirds of the states, and 200,000,000 of 300,000,000 Americans are ignored in presidential elections.[42]

Moreover, this concentrated attention does not apparently end with the election. Writing in *The Rise of the President's Permanent Campaign*, political scientist Brendan Doherty noted that recent Presidents have spent a disproportionate amount of time visiting identified battleground states during their first term of office.[43]

Alleged Biases and Advantages of the Electoral College System

Critics of the electoral college often point to what they characterize as "biases" in the system: inherent constitutional provisions or political arrangements that tend to favor various states or classes of voter in the presidential election process. During the 1960s and 1970s, several of these biases were identified and widely debated when electoral college reform proposals were actively considered by Congress. Three particular phenomena were identified: the arithmetic advantage

---

[39] Michael Barone, "States Aren't Red or Blue Forever," *The American* (American Enterprise Institute), March 13, 2012, available at http://www.american.com/archive/2012/march/states-arent-red-or-blue-forever.

[40] Ibid.

[41] A wide range of news organizations monitor and report on trends in battleground and other states during the presidential election. For example, see "2012 Swing States," *Politico*," at http://www.politico.com/2012-election/swing-state/; or "The Electoral Map: Building a Path to Victory," *New York Times*, at http://elections.nytimes.com/2012/electoral-map.

[42] "Pundits Already Say Only 7-14 States Will Matter in 2012," National Popular Vote web site, available at: http://www.nationalpopularvote.com/pages/misc/hl_20110514_7-14-states-matter-2012.php. For further information on the National Popular Vote plan, see in this report under "Reform Through State or Non-Governmental Alternatives."

[43] Brendan J. Doherty, *The Rise of the President's Permanent Campaign* (Lawrence, KS: University of Kansas Press, 2012), pp. 113-114.

enjoyed by less populous states, due to the allocation of two "senatorial" electors to all states regardless of population; the "voting power" advantage enjoyed by voters in populous states due to the leverage provided by the general ticket winner-take-all method; and an asserted advantage enjoyed by minority voters concentrated in the same populous states, whose voting patterns can shift results in these states therein, and thereby exert a greater influence on the election.

Small State Arithmetic Advantage

As the composition of the electoral college is based on state representation in Congress, some maintain it is inconsistent with the "one person, one vote" principle.[44] As noted earlier in this report, the Constitutional Convention of 1787 agreed on a compromise election plan whereby less populous states were assured of a minimum of three electoral votes, based on two Senators and one Representative, regardless of state population. Since state electoral college delegations are equal to the combined total of each state's Senate and House delegation, the composition of the electoral college thus appears to be weighted in favor of the small states. The two "senatorial" electors and the one "representative" elector to which each state is entitled may confer an advantage on smaller states over more populous ones because voters in the smaller states, in effect, cast more electoral votes per voter. For instance, in 2008, voters in Wyoming, the least populous state, cast 254,658 popular votes and three electoral votes for President, or one electoral vote for every 84,873 voters. By comparison, Californians cast 13,561,900 popular votes and 55 electoral votes, or one electoral vote for every 246,580.[45] As a result of this distribution of electoral votes among the states, it is argued that "small" states have an advantage over large states with regard to electoral vote allocation relative to their populations.

Large State Voting Power Advantage

While it is generally recognized that small states possess an arithmetical advantage in the electoral college, some observers hold that, conversely, the most populous (large) states enjoy a "voting power" advantage, because they control the largest blocs of electoral votes. For example, voters in more populous states are better able to influence a larger bloc of electoral votes than those in less populous ones, because of the winner-take-all method of allocating electoral votes. Thus, to use the previously cited examples, a voter in Wyoming in 2008 could influence only three electoral votes, 1.1% of the 270 needed to win the presidency, whereas a voter in California could influence 55 electoral votes, comprising 20.4% of the necessary majority of electoral votes in the same presidential election. According to this argument, known as the "voting power" theory, the electoral college system actually provides an *advantage* to the six most populous states (California, 55 electoral votes; Texas, 38, electoral votes; Florida and New York, 29 electoral votes; and Illinois and Pennsylvania, 20 electoral votes each) and disadvantages all other states and the District of Columbia.[46]

---

[44] The one person, one vote principle was established by the U.S. Supreme Court in congressional and state legislative reapportionment and redistricting cases in order to insure equal representation for equal numbers of people. *See, e.g., Reynolds v. Sims,* 377 U.S. 533, 568 (1964) and *Wesberry v. Sanders,* 376 U.S. 1, 7-18 (1964).

[45] Computed by CRS from "2008 Election Results," *CQ 2008 Almanac* (Washington: Congressional Quarterly, Inc., 2009) p. 10-8.

[46] Peirce and Longley, *The People's President,* pp. 119-127. Lawrence D. Longley and James D. Dana, Jr., *The Biases of the Electoral College in the 1990s,* 25 Polity 123-45 (1992).

Large State Ethnic/Minority Voter Advantage

Another theory advanced during debate on electoral college reform in the 1960s and 1970s, centered on the asserted advantage enjoyed by ethnic minority voters, which combines their voting patterns and their tendency to be concentrated in more populous states. According to this argument, minority voters (e.g., African Americans, Latinos, and Jews) tend to reside and vote in populous states with large electoral college delegations. By virtue of this concentration, they are presumably able to exert greater influence over the outcomes in such states because their voting patterns tend strongly to favor candidates whose policies they perceive to be favorable to their interests, thus helping to gain these states and their electoral votes for the favored candidates. According to this theory, since these more populous states enjoy purported "voting power" advantages, the influence of minority and ethnic voters is still further magnified. These arguments were advanced by the Presidents of the American Jewish Congress and the National Urban League as reasons for their support of the electoral college system during hearings before the Senate Judiciary Committee's Subcommittee on the Constitution as it considered a direct election amendment in 1979.[47]

"Mend It" — Reforming the Electoral College

Two alternative methods for awarding electoral votes that pass the test of constitutionality have long been available to the states, the district and proportional plans. They have historically been promoted as avoiding the alleged failings of the general ticket system, and, according to their advocates, they have an added virtue in that they would not require a constitutional amendment. A third reform option, the automatic plan, would, however, require a constitutional amendment.

The District Plan

The district plan or system, as noted in the summary of this report, has been adopted by Maine and Nebraska. Under this arrangement, the voters in each state choose two electors on a statewide, at-large basis (representing the two "senatorial electors" allotted to each state regardless of population), and one elector in each congressional district.[48] Each voter still casts a single vote for President and Vice President, but the votes are counted twice: first on a statewide basis, where the two at-large elector-candidates who win the most votes (a plurality is sufficient) are both elected, and then again in each district, where the district elector-candidate who receives the most votes in each district (again, a plurality is sufficient) is elected.

This is how the district plan might work in State A, which, as noted earlier, is apportioned eight Representatives in Congress, and thus, when its two "senatorial" electors are added, has a 10-member electoral college delegation. Assume that Party X receives 51% of the statewide vote,

---

[47] U.S. Congress, Senate, Committee on the Judiciary, Subcommittee on the Constitution, *Direct Election of the President and Vice President of the United States*, hearings on S.J.Res. 28, 96th Cong., 1st ess., March 27, 30 April 3, 9, 1979 (Washington: GPO, 1979), pp. 163-219. The validity of these assertions was, however, questioned by Peirce and Longley in *The People's President*. Writing of conditions in the 1970s, they maintained that the electoral college system actually disadvantaged African American voters. See *The People's President*, pp. 127-130.

[48] Some versions of the district plan would use ad hoc presidential election districts to award these votes, rather than congressional districts, but both Maine and Nebraska, which use the district system, tally their votes by congressional district.

---

and Party Y, 49%. Party X's candidates for the two statewide (or senatorial) elector offices are thus elected. Assume also that Party X receives a plurality or majority of the popular vote in five of State A's eight congressional districts, while Party Y wins in the other three districts. Under the District Plan, the "district" electoral votes would be similarly awarded, so that Party X would receive the five district votes, which when added to the senatorial electors, would total seven electors, while Party Y would receive the three electors that reflected its congressional district majorities.

The claimed advantage of the district plan is that it is said to more accurately reflect differences in support in various parts of a state, and does not necessarily "disenfranchise" voters who picked the losing ticket. For instance, a state that has one or more large cities whose residents tend to support one party, and a large rural or suburban population with differing political preferences and voting patterns, might well split its electoral vote under the district system. Opponents suggest that the district plan, with its division of electoral votes within states, would more frequently lead to deadlocked elections in which no candidate receives a majority of electoral votes.

Maine has never split its electoral vote during the time the district plan has been in place, but Nebraska did so for the first time in 2008.[49] The Cornhusker state split its district votes, awarding four electors to Republican candidates Senator John McCain and Alaska Governor Sarah Palin, who won two congressional districts and the statewide vote, and one to the Democratic nominees, Senators Barack Obama and Joseph Biden, who received the most popular votes in the state's Second Congressional District.[50]

For the record, had the district plan been in place nationwide for the 2008 presidential election, the electoral vote tally would have been different, but the results would have remained unchanged. Under the current plan, the Obama/Biden ticket won 52.9% of the popular vote and 365 electoral votes, 67.8% of the electoral vote total. McCain/Palin won 45.7% of the popular vote, and 173 electoral votes, 32.2% of the electoral vote total.[51] Under the district plan, Obama/Biden would have won 301 (55.9%) electoral votes to 237 (44.1%) for McCain/Palin.[52] As its proponents claim, the allocation of electoral votes under the district plan, at least in 2008, would have more closely approximated the percentage of the popular vote won by the two major party tickets.

The Proportional Plan

The other commonly proposed option is the proportional plan or system, which has never been adopted by a state, but was the subject of a proposed Colorado constitutional amendment that was rejected by that state's voters in the 2004 general election. The proportional plan allocates

---

[49] The District Plan became operative in Maine for the presidential election of 1972, and in Nebraska, for the election of 1992.

[50] Nebraska, Secretary of State, *Official Results of Nebraska General Election, November 4, 2008*, "Federal Offices: For President of the United States by Congressional District," pp. 10-11. Available at http://www.sos.ne.gov/elec/pdf/ 2008%20General%20Canvass%20Book.pdf.

[51] U.S., Federal Election Commission, *2008 Official General Presidential Election Results*, January 9, 2009. Available at http://www.fec.gov/pubrec/fe2008/2008presgeresults.pdf.

[52] Results computed by CRS. Data on District Plan electoral vote allocation for the 1992, 1996, 2000, and 2004 presidential elections are available to Members of Congress and congressional staff from the author of this report.

electors and electoral votes in direct proportion to the number of votes won by each ticket of candidates. Unlike the district plan, it does not account for geographical voting patterns within a state, but allocates electors on a purely statewide basis. Two variations exist: the *strict* proportional plan, that would allocate electoral votes to thousandths of electoral votes, that is, to the third decimal point, and the *rounded* proportional plan, that would use some method of rounding to allocate only whole electoral votes.

This is how the rounded proportional plan might operate in State A, with its 10 electoral votes. For this case, assume Party X receives 59.679% of the popular vote, and Party Y receives 40.321%. When these totals are rounded, Party X would be awarded six electors, and Party Y would gain four.[53]

Proponents of the proportional system argue that this is the fairest plan, since it most accurately reflects in its elector/electoral vote allocation the preferences of the voters, acting as a statewide political community. They also note that it would provide recognition for new-party or third-party candidates that achieve a substantial level of support in a state. Opponents suggest that because the proportional plan also splits a state's electoral votes among various candidates, it could, like the district plan, lead to deadlocked elections in which no candidate receives a majority of electoral votes nationwide.

For the record, had a rounded proportional plan been in place nationwide for the 2008 presidential election, the electoral vote tally would have been different, but the results would have remained unchanged. As noted earlier, under the current plan, the Obama/Biden ticket won 52.9% of the popular vote and 365 electoral votes, which comprises 67.8% of the electoral vote total. McCain/Palin won 45.7% of the popular vote, and 173 electoral votes, or 32.2% of the electoral vote total.[54] Under the rounded proportional plan, Obama/Biden would have won 288 electoral votes, 53.5% of the total, to 249 votes, 46.3% of the total, for McCain/Palin. One electoral vote, from California, would have been awarded to Peace and Freedom Party candidates Ralph Nader and Matt Gonzales.[55] As with district plan, the allocation of electoral votes under the Proportional Plan in 2008 would have more closely approximated the percentage of the popular vote won by the two major party tickets.

The Automatic Plan

The automatic plan or system comes closest to replicating the current "winner-take-all," or "general ticket" system by which the winning candidates in a state take all the state's electors and electoral votes. Most versions of this proposal also eliminate the office of presidential elector, and award electoral votes directly to candidates who won the most popular votes (generally, a plurality) in a particular state. Unlike the district and rounded proportional plans, however, the automatic plan would require a constitutional amendment, because it would abolish the office of presidential elector.

---

[53] Given that the strict proportional plan, by providing for fractions of electoral votes, would almost certainly require a U.S. constitutional amendment, and since the proposed Colorado constitutional amendment proposed a rounded proportional system, this method of allocating of electoral votes has not been included in this illustration.

[54] U.S., Federal Election Commission, *2008 Official General Presidential Election Results*, January 9, 2009. Available at http://www.fec.gov/pubrec/fe2008/2008presgeresults.pdf.

[55] Results computed by CRS. Data on Proportional Plan electoral vote allocation for the 1992, 1996, and 2000 presidential elections are available to Members of Congress and congressional staff from the author of this report.

Supporters claim it preserves what they consider to be some of the advantages of the existing system: first, they assert, it would continue to deliver all of a state's electoral votes to the winning candidates, thus contributing to decisive results in presidential elections; they claim it would also help maintain an ideologically broad and stable two-party political system. Opponents maintain that it would continue to "disenfranchise" voters who picked the losing candidates by using the winner-take-all device, and that, in common with other proposed electoral college reforms, it would not guarantee that the candidates winning the most popular votes would always be elected.

Reform Through State or Non-Governmental Alternatives

Constitutional amendments that would revise electoral college procedures or eliminate the system altogether are routinely introduced in every Congress. The obstacles faced by would-be constitutional amendments are considerable, however: they requires two-thirds approval in both houses of Congress, and ratification by three-fourths of the states, usually within a period of seven years. Although there were a number of noteworthy attempts to reform the electoral college system or replace it with direct popular election in the three decades following 1949, there has been no floor action in Congress on any related proposals since 1979, and the most recent hearings were held in 1992. In recent years, measures to change the nation's presidential election system are increasingly likely to have originated on the state level, or be offered by non-governmental organizations. These have included

- Colorado Amendment 36, a rounded proportional plan initiative that was rejected by the state's voters in 2004;

- the California Presidential Reform Act (California Counts), a district plan proposal that failed to win ballot access in that state in 2008; and

- National Popular Vote, Inc., a campaign organized by a non-governmental public interest organization to promote an interstate compact under which participating states would agree to award their electoral votes to the nationwide popular vote winner.[56]

"End It" — Replacing the Electoral College with Direct Popular Election

The most widely introduced proposal to reform the presidential election system would scrap the electoral college altogether and replace it with direct popular election of the President and Vice President. Most direct election proposals provide that the joint ticket of candidates for President and Vice President that wins the most popular vote — a plurality would be sufficient — would be elected. Some versions of direct popular election would require candidates to gain at least 40% of

---

[56] Briefly, the National Popular Vote initiative (NPV) is an interstate compact or agreement by which each participating state agrees to cast its electoral votes for the candidates winning the most popular votes nationwide, whether or not those candidates won the most popular votes within the state. NPV's constitutional authority rests on the Constitution's broad grant of authority over the appointment of electors to the states. NPV will not take effect unless or until states that dispose of a majority of electoral votes, 270 or more, have agreed to the compact. For additional information on the National Popular Vote Plan, please see CRS Report R42139, *Contemporary Developments in Presidential Elections*, by Kevin J. Coleman, R. Sam Garrett, and Thomas H. Neale.

the vote in order to win; generally these proposals would provide for a runoff election or election by Congress if the necessary percentage is not gained.

Proponents of direct popular election argue that it is simple, democratic, and foolproof: the candidates with the most popular votes would win under any conceivable circumstance.[57] Opponents, and defenders of the electoral college, claim that the existing system is an integral and vital element in the U.S. federal system, that it contributes to a stable and ideologically diverse two party system, and that it has delivered the "people's choice"[58] in 47 of 51 presidential elections since the 12th Amendment came into effect in 1804—what they characterize as an excellent track record.[59]

For further information on mending or ending the electoral college, please consult CRS Report R42139, *Contemporary Developments in Presidential Elections*, by Kevin J. Coleman, R. Sam Garrett, and Thomas H. Neale.

Concluding Observations

The electoral college system has demonstrated both durability and adaptability during more than two centuries of government under the U.S. Constitution. Although its constitutional elements have remained largely unchanged since ratification of the 12th Amendment, the electoral college has never worked quite the way the founders anticipated: as an indirect, deliberate selection process, carefully filtered from political considerations. Instead, it accommodated the demands of an increasingly democratic and political-party dominated presidential election system, ultimately evolving into a patchwork assemblage of constitutional provisions, state laws, political party practices, and enduring traditions that, with several notable exceptions, has delivered the popular vote winners in most presidential elections. Given the high hurdles faced by proposed constitutional amendments, it seems likely to remain in place unless or until its alleged failings become so compelling that large concurrent majorities in the public, Congress, and the states, are prepared to undertake its reform or abolition.

In recent years, potential alternatives to constitutional change have emerged on the state level, and even in non-governmental advocacy campaigns, and it is arguable that these state and "grass roots" movements may have greater chances for success than a constitutional amendment. As noted earlier in this report, Colorado's Amendment 36 initiative was rejected at the polls in 2004, and the politically controversial "California Counts" initiative proposal failed to attain ballot access in the latter state in 2008. It is arguable, however, that the interest generated by such efforts may stimulate further experimentation in alternative electoral college plans, in which the states might serve in their classic role as "laboratories" for national policy. Moreover, the most notably successful electoral college reform effort in recent decades has been both non-federal and, in its origins, non-governmental. The National Popular Vote campaign, cited earlier in this report, has enjoyed a degree of success, having been approved in eight states (and the District of

---

[57] The only exceptions might occur under variations that call for election by Congress in the event of a tie, or if no candidate receives a requisite minimum of votes, e.g. 40%.

[58] In this case, the "people's choice" is defined as the candidate or candidates who won a majority or plurality of *popular* votes.

[59] For more detailed information on reform proposals, please consult CRS Report R42139, *Contemporary Developments in Presidential Elections*, by Kevin J. Coleman, R. Sam Garrett, and Thomas H. Neale.

Columbia) that collectively control 132 electoral votes.[60] It has also been passed by one or both legislative chambers, but not gained final approval, in a number of additional states. Here again, however, the ultimate fate of the electoral college system arguably rests on the results it produces: in modern times, the college is expected to ratify the public choice by delivering the presidency to the candidates who have gained the most popular votes. If the electoral college system meets expectations, these proposals may languish. If it does not, they or others like them could attract sufficient popular and political support to become viable alternatives.

---

[60] At the time of this writing, the following jurisdictions, in chronological order, have joined the National Popular Vote compact: Hawaii, 2008, 4 electoral votes; Illinois, 2008, 20 electoral votes; Maryland, 2008, 10 electoral votes; New Jersey, 2008, 14 electoral votes; Washington, 2009, 12 electoral votes; Massachusetts, 2010, 11 electoral votes; the District of Columbia, 2010, 3 electoral votes; Vermont, 2011, 3 electoral votes; California, 2011, 55 electoral votes.

Appendix. Electoral Vote Allocation by States and the District of Columbia

Figure A-1. Map of State Electoral Vote Allocations, Presidential Elections of 2012, 2016, and 2020

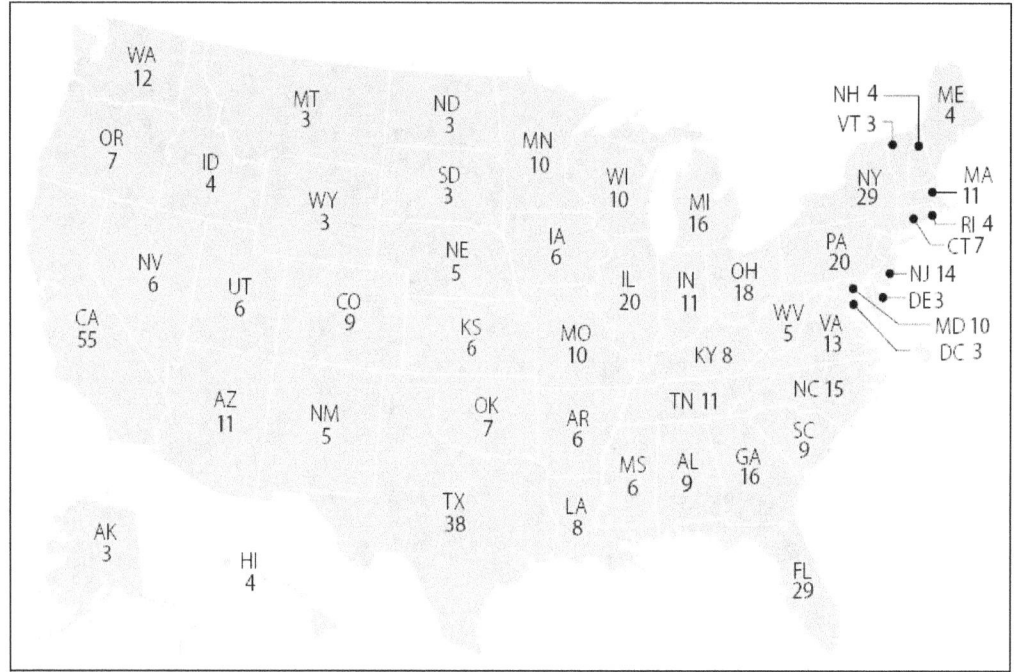

Source: Compiled by the Congressional Research Service

Table A-1. Electoral Vote Allocation by States and the District of Columbia, Presidential Elections of 2012, 2016, and 2020

State	Electors	State	Electors	State	Electors
Alabama	9	Kentucky	8	North Dakota	3
Alaska	3	Louisiana	8	Ohio	18
Arizona	11	Maine	4	Oklahoma	7
Arkansas	6	Maryland	10	Oregon	7
California	55	Massachusetts	11	Pennsylvania	20
Colorado	9	Michigan	16	Rhode Island	4
Connecticut	7	Minnesota	10	South Carolina	9
Delaware	3	Mississippi	6	South Dakota	3
District of Columbia	3	Missouri	10	Tennessee	11

State	Electors	State	Electors	State	Electors
Florida	29	Montana	3	Texas	38
Georgia	16	Nebraska	5	Utah	6
Hawaii	4	Nevada	6	Vermont	3
Idaho	4	New Hampshire	4	Virginia	13
Illinois	20	New Jersey	14	Washington	12
Indiana	11	New Mexico	5	West Virginia	5
Iowa	6	New York	29	Wisconsin	10
Kansas	6	North Carolina	15	Wyoming	3

Source: Compiled by the Congressional Research Service.

Author Contact Information

Thomas H. Neale
Specialist in American National Government
tneale@crs.loc.gov, 7-7883